Fierce Fighters
AZTEC WARRIORS

Charlotte Guillain

www.raintreepublishers.co.uk
Visit our website to find out
more information about
Raintree books.

To order:
☎ Phone 0845 6044371
🖷 Fax +44 (0) 1865 312263
🖳 Email myorders@raintreepublishers.co.uk

Customers from outside the UK please telephone +44 1865 312262

Raintree is an imprint of Capstone Global Library Limited,
a company incorporated in England and Wales having its
registered office at 7 Pilgrim Street, London, EC4V 6LB
– Registered company number: 6695582

Text © Capstone Global Library Limited 2010
First published in hardback in 2010
Paperback edition first published in 2011
The moral rights of the proprietor have been asserted.

Edited by Rebecca Rissman, Nancy Dickmann, and
Catherine Veitch
Designed by Joanna Hinton-Malivoire
Picture research by Tracy Cummins
Original illlustrations © Capstone Global Library 2010
Original illustrations by Miracle Studios
Production by Victoria Fitzgerald
Originated by Capstone Global Library
Printed and bound in China by Leo Paper Products

ISBN 978 1 40621 616 5 (hardback)
14 13 12 11 10
10 9 8 7 6 5 4 3 2 1

ISBN 978 1 40621 638 7 (paperback)
15 14 13 12 11
10 9 8 7 6 5 4 3 2 1

British Library Cataloguing in Publication Data
Guillain, Charlotte.
Aztec warriors. -- (Fierce fighters)
355.1'0972-dc22

Acknowledgements
We would like to thank the following for permission to
reproduce photographs: Art Resource, NY p. **12** (© The
Trustees of The British Museum), akg-images pp. **14**, **19**;
Alamy p. **24** (© Hannamariah); Corbis p. **25** (© Historical
Picture Archive); Getty Images pp. **17** (Moritz Steiger),
20 (Hulton Archive); Heinemann Raintree pp. **28 top**
(Karon Dubke), **28 bottom** (Karon Dubke), **29 top**
(Karon Dubke), **29 middle** (Karon Dubke), **29 bottom**
(Karon Dubke); Shutterstock pp. **13** (© Matty Symons),
18 (© Hannamariah); The Art Archive pp. **6** (Bodleian
Library Oxford), **9**, **10** (Museo Ciudad Mexico / Alfredo
Dagli Orti), **11**, **22** (Museum für Völkerkunde Vienna /
Gianni Dagli Orti); The Granger Collection, New York
pp. **21**, **23**.

Front cover illustration of Aztecs fighting the Spanish
reproduced with permission of Miracle Studios.

The publishers would like to thank Jane Penrose for her
assistance in the preparation of this book.

**Some words are shown in bold, like this. You can find
out what they mean by looking in the glossary.**

Contents

Winning warriors

Place: City in Mexico
Date: 1400s

The city is on fire. The streets are empty and most people are dead. The only sound is the noise of marching **warriors**. They are leaving the city with **prisoners**.

The Aztec warriors have won another war!

Aztec timeline

1200s	Aztecs arrive in Mexico
1400s	Aztec Empire is powerful
1500s	Spain takes over Aztec Empire
1600s	People from Europe start to settle in North America
2000s	You are reading this book

Who were the Aztecs?

The Aztecs lived in the land that is now Mexico. Aztecs loved war! Their fierce **warriors** took land to build an **empire**.

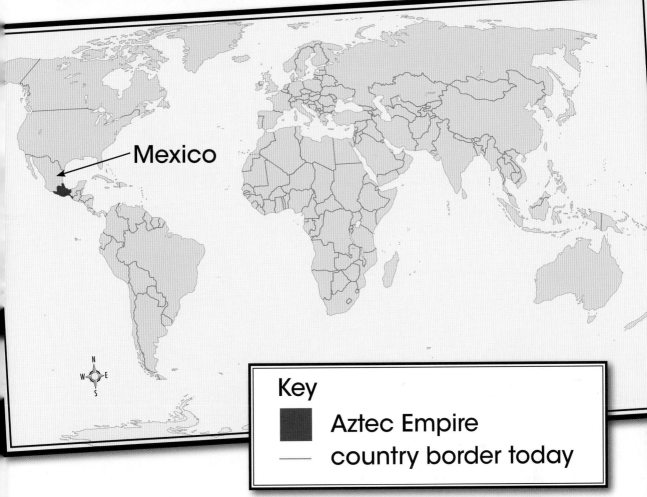

Mexico

Key

■ Aztec Empire

----- country border today

DID YOU KNOW?

Mexico City is the **capital city** of Mexico today. It stands in the same place as the Aztecs first built their city.

Becoming an Aztec warrior

Most Aztec boys wanted to be **warriors** when they grew up. Baby boys played with toy weapons. When they got older they learned to fight and take **prisoners**.

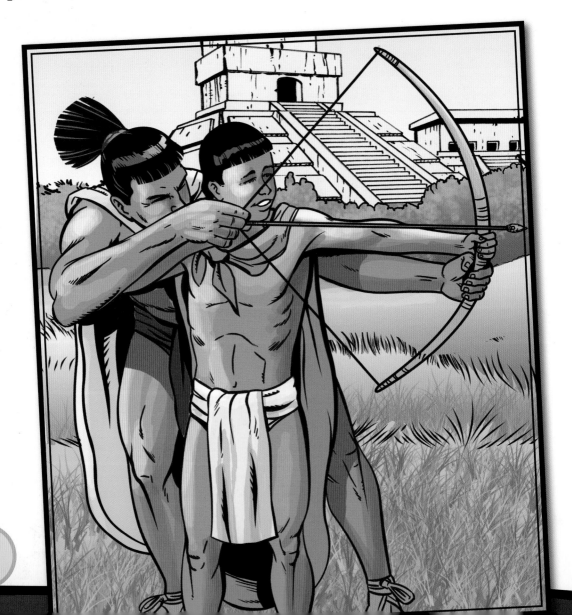

DID YOU KNOW?

If Aztec children were naughty, they were punished. Some had to lie in a muddy puddle all day. Others were pricked with spikes from a cactus.

Prisoners

Warriors tried to take many **prisoners**. Then they could become **Jaguar** or **Eagle** warriors. These warriors wore jaguar skins or eagle's head helmets. They led many other warriors.

Eagle warrior

TLACATECUHTLI TEQUIHUA CALPIXQUE

TOLTECA MAYEQUE TLAMEME TLACOTLI

Jaguar warrior

teçiquauhtitlã

Only the best fighters could become Jaguar or Eagle warriors.

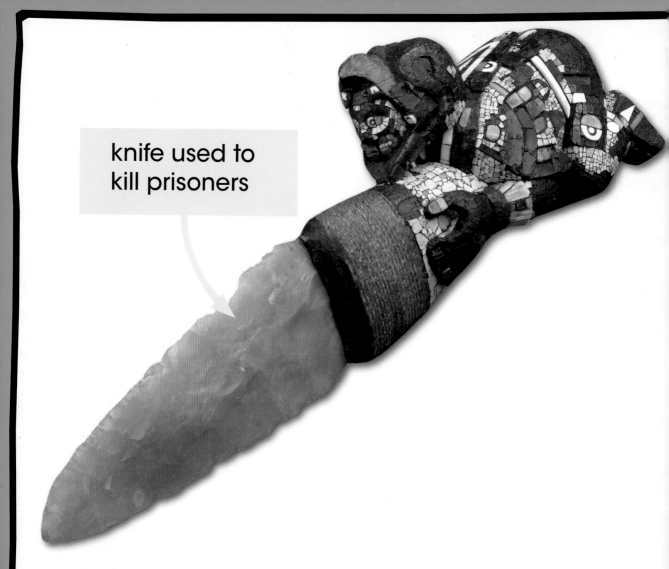

knife used to
kill prisoners

Aztec **warriors** took **prisoners** so they
could kill them later. They wanted to
kill prisoners in a **temple** for the god
of war. The Aztecs thought this would
make the god happy. Then he would
help them win more wars.

This wall carving shows a different kind of sacrifice. A priest has just cut off someone's head!

priest

head

13

Aztec weapons

Aztec **warriors** threw **spears** at their enemies. Some warriors hit their enemies with stone **clubs** with sharp edges. This could knock someone's head off!

club

14

spear

DID YOU KNOW?
Sometimes Aztec warriors used swords to slice off their enemies' ears.

Aztec **warriors** carried large shields to **protect** themselves. They covered their shields and clothes in animal fur and feathers. This made them look very fierce.

shield

DID YOU KNOW?

Aztec soldiers wore different coloured feathers to show how important they were. For example, an **emperor** wore red feathers. An emperor was a leader.

Death

Aztecs believed how they died decided what happened to them after death. They believed **warriors** became butterflies or hummingbirds and followed the Sun to heaven.

DID YOU KNOW?

Aztecs thought the **prisoners** they killed would go straight to heaven.

Aztec warrior kings

All new Aztec kings started a war to show everyone how strong they were. Moctezuma I (say *mos-tes-uma*) was a great king and **warrior**. His armies took many cities.

Moctezuma I

DID YOU KNOW?

Moctezuma's middle name Ilhuicamina (say *il-hue-sa-mina*) meant "he shoots an arrow into the sky".

Ahuizotl (say *ah-wit-sot-ul*) was another fierce **warrior** king. He was a strong leader and built a huge **empire**. He had the same name as a fierce animal in Aztec stories.

This shield shows the Ahuizotl animal.

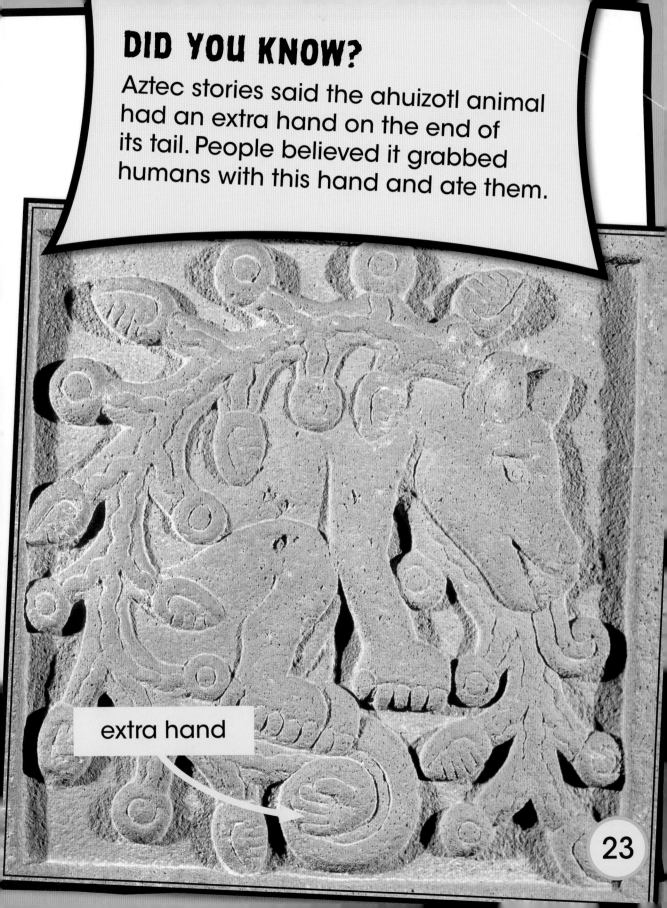

DID YOU KNOW?

Aztec stories said the ahuizotl animal had an extra hand on the end of its tail. People believed it grabbed humans with this hand and ate them.

extra hand

Aztec women

Aztec women had to feed the hungry **warriors**. They also made clothes and looked after children. Aztec people thought women who died having babies were as brave as warriors. They thought these women would go straight to heaven.

This carving shows an Aztec mother with her child.

DID YOU KNOW?

Aztec girls usually got married between the ages of 12 and 15.

The end of the Aztecs

In 1519 a Spanish army came to the Aztec **Empire**. The Aztecs thought the Spanish leader was a god. The Spanish took the Aztec king Moctezuma II **prisoner** and attacked the Aztec army. The Aztec Empire was finished.

DID YOU KNOW?

The Spanish brought diseases, such as smallpox. Many Aztecs got sick and died.

Aztec activity

Make an Aztec warrior's feather shield

You will need:
- a circle of thick card - the **diameter** should be around the same length as your arm
- different coloured tissue paper
- pencil
- paints
- PVA glue

1. Draw a picture of a fierce animal in the centre of your shield and paint it.

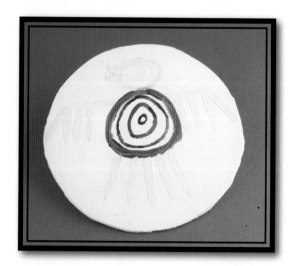

2. Tear the tissue paper into thin, feather-like shreds. Glue the tissue paper "feathers" around your picture.

3. Attach a strip of card to the back so you can hold your shield.

You are ready to go into battle!

Glossary

capital city city where the people who rule a country work

club heavy stick, used as a weapon

diameter widest distance across a circle

eagle large bird with a hooked beak and sharp claws

emperor ruler of a large area

empire large area ruled by a king or emperor

jaguar big cat living in forests of Central and South America

prisoner person kept in a jail or prison

spear weapon with sharp point on a long pole

temple building used for religious ceremonies

warrior fighter

Find out more

Books

Aztec Warriors, Mary Englar
(Capstone Edge Books, 2008)

Blood and Celebration: Aztec Beliefs, Heidi Moore
(Raintree Fusion, 2008)

Time Travel Guide: The Aztec Empire, Jane Bingham
(Heinemann/Raintree, 2008)

Websites

www.mexicolore.co.uk
Mexicolore is a website full of information about the
Aztecs and Mexico. Look at the Aztec pages for lots of
facts and activities.

www.pbs.org/wnet/nature/spirits/html/body_aztec.html
This website has lots more information about the Aztecs.

Places to visit

The British Museum, London
www.britishmuseum.org/
Find out more about the Aztecs at the British Museum.

Find out

What would you
find in every Aztec
kitchen?

Index